LIZ WATSON

NETBALL LEGENDS

First published by Albert Street Books, an imprint of Allen & Unwin, in 2025

Allen & Unwin
Cammeraygal Country
83 Alexander Street
Crows Nest NSW 2065
Australia
Phone: (61 2) 8425 0100
Email: info@allenandunwin.com
Web: www.allenandunwin.com

Allen & Unwin acknowledges the Traditional Owners of the Country on which we live and work. We pay our respects to all Aboriginal and Torres Strait Islander Elders, past and present.

A catalogue record for this book is available from the National Library of Australia

ISBN 978 1 76118 173 3

For teaching resources, explore allenandunwin.com/learn

Cover design by Hana Kinoshita Thomson
Cover photo by PA Images / Alamy Stock Photo
Text design by Hana Kinoshita Thomson
Set in 14 pt Urbane Rounded Medium
Printed and bound in Australia by the Opus Group

10 9 8 7 6 5 4 3 2 1

KIT CROSS

LEIGH HEDSTROM

WA

LIZ WATSON

NETBALL LEGENDS

CONTENTS

CHAPTER 1: Legendary Liz 1

CHAPTER 2: Born to Play 11

CHAPTER 3: Finding Her Footwork 21

CHAPTER 4: Midcourt Magic 31

CHAPTER 5: Shooting for the Stars 41

CHAPTER 6: We Are the Vixens! 51

CHAPTER 7: Netball Know-how 61

CHAPTER 8: Diamonds Are Forever 75

CHAPTER 9: Going for Gold 93

CHAPTER 10: The Road Ahead 109

CHAPTER ONE

LEGENDARY LIZ

Hi there. I'm Gary the G.O.A.T.

I may not be the **Greatest. Of. All. Time,** but I do have a winning streak in sports trivia!

Just call me **G-GOAT (Greatest Grandmaster Of Athletic Things).**

But you know who *is* an actual

HONEST-TO-GOODNESS LEGEND?

Netball player LIZ WATSON

And this book is all about her!

Liz is considered one of the best **attacking midcourters** in the world, and she has the

SKILLS

to back it up!

She is **FAST** and **AGILE,** delivering pinpoint passes and helping get the ball down the court.

She is **SHARP** and **TACTICAL,** always one step ahead and creating **opportunities** for her team.

She is a **LEADER,** supporting teammates, staying positive and leading by example.

LIZ'S
LEGENDARY
SKILLS:
Pivots
Stamina
WA
Intercepts
Hand-eye co-ordination
Chest pass and bounce pass
Agility

'Netball has given me many skills to be a **strong** and **confident** person in my everyday life, to make really good choices and be confident in my **ability.**'

LIZ WATSON

WHAT MAKES LIZ SUCH A LEGEND ON THE COURT?

STRATEGY & VISION

Her **decision-making skills** and **court vision** allow her to spot gaps in the defence and set up **valuable scoring opportunities.**

MIDCOURT DOMINANCE

As a **midcourt player,** she helps link defence to attack and is known for **always being in the right place at the right time.**

PASSING ACCURACY

Her **quick, precise passes** help her team keep possession of the ball.

ENDURANCE & AGILITY

Liz is **fast, agile** and **incredibly fit,** and her **ability to change direction instantly** makes her nearly impossible to defend against.

MENTAL TOUGHNESS

She has **battled through injuries** and setbacks, but **always comes back stronger.**

Name:
Elizabeth Bruna Watson

Date of Birth:
30 March 1994

Place of Birth:
Melbourne, VIC
(Naarm, Kulin Nation)

Height:
1.78m

Nicknames:
Lizzy, Watto

Position:
Wing Attack (WA) and Centre (C)

Diamond Number:
168

Clubs: Manchester City WFC , Montpellier HSC, Bankstown City FC, Illawarra Stingrays, Adelaide United

National team: Australian Diamonds

CHAPTER TWO

BORN TO PLAY

Liz Watson was born in 1994 in **Carlton, Victoria.**

Carlton is an inner suburb of **Melbourne/Naarm,** well-known for its **Italian cafes** and **restaurants,** its **Victorian heritage** streets and buildings, and its leafy parks and gardens.

Did you know the **Royal Exhibition Building** and **Carlton Gardens** were added to the **World Heritage List** in **2004**?

Liz is the daughter of **Manuela** and **Neil Watson,** and she has **two brothers.**

Her family is full of very sporty people! Her mum played **state league netball,** and her two uncles, **Anthony** and **Steven Alessio,** and her older brother, **Matthew,** are all former **Australian Rules footballers.**

'Every **family occasion** was spent outside playing **footy.** I'm the only younger female on my mum's side of the family, so had to mix it with my dad and uncles, cousins and brothers. They say they've made me **tougher** and **more competitive** – they take that credit.'

LIZ WATSON

Growing up in a **sports-loving family,** Liz was used to being **active** from an early age. She played a **range of sports** as a child, such as...

FOOTY

SWIMMING

BASKETBALL

ATHLETICS

She even **competed at the state level** in some of these sports.

But it was
NETBALL
that captured
her heart!

Liz first played netball at **St Fidelis Primary School** after her best friend encouraged her to join the team. She took part in **inter-school netball competitions,** which sparked her **love for the game.**

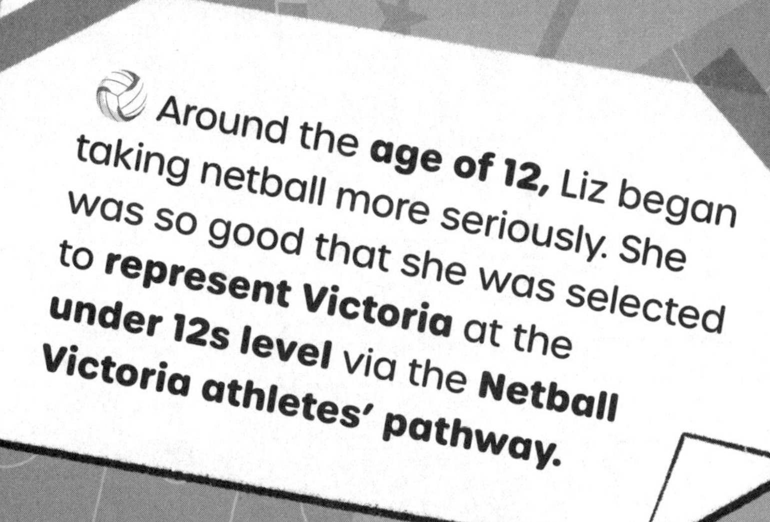

Around the **age of 12,** Liz began taking netball more seriously. She was so good that she was selected to **represent Victoria** at the **under 12s level** via the **Netball Victoria athletes' pathway.**

When Liz's mum, Manuela, played state level netball, her position was Goal Defence (GD).

Manuela is tall, and her main job as GD was to defend the ball and stop the opposite team from scoring.

She doesn't play as much these days, but she loves to watch her daughter on the court and even helped teach Liz how to play!

CHAPTER THREE

FINDING HER FOOTWORK

After primary school, Liz went to

PENLEIGH AND ESSENDON GRAMMAR SCHOOL (PEGS)

and joined the

AND

ATHLETICS TEAM

in her first year.

She was a **natural competitor,** balancing **fast footwork** on the netball court with **powerful sprints** on the track. In Years 10 and 11, Liz kept up her **passion** for netball and athletics.

Then came **Year 12, her biggest year yet!**

Liz was chosen as

of the **PEGS Firsts Netball Team,** leading her school with

She also captained the **Associated Grammar Schools Victoria (AGSV) Representative Team** in their big showdown against the **Associated Public Schools of Victoria (APS).**

Liz was on her way to becoming a **sporting superstar,** but did you know her **favourite subject** at school was **Art?**

Junior clubs are the **first taste of competitive netball** for a lot of young players. These clubs are an **excellent training ground** because you learn about important things like…

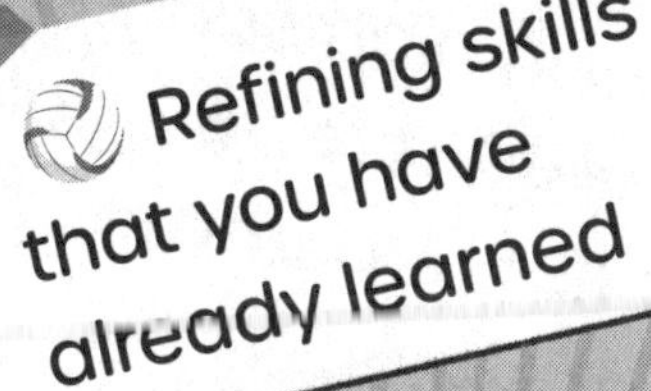

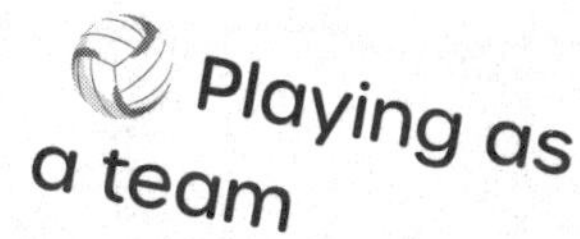

Commitment to the game

Good sporting behaviour

The emphasis is on **having fun,** and **winning is a bonus!**

While she was in high school, Liz **represented Victoria** again in the **under 15s** and **under 17s state competitions.**

Playing so many games gave Liz the chance to not only sharpen her **speed** and **teamwork skills,** but also figure out **which position suited her best.**

‘Growing up playing netball I tried all positions, but **GA was my favourite.** It wasn’t until I was about 17 that I moved more into the **midcourt** playing **WA** and **C.**’
LIZ WATSON

Liz loves **sport,**
but she also loves
art and **reading!**

Her **favourite books** were by
ROALD DAHL.

They were always the first ones she would **borrow from her school library.**

CHAPTER FOUR

MID-COURT MAGIC

Liz didn't just play netball – she

it at **every level!**

In **2012,** Liz was part of the

Victorian under 19 team

that won the

AUSTRALIAN NATIONAL NETBALL CHAMPIONSHIPS!

The very next year, she stepped up to the **under 21 team** and made it to the **grand final.** Her team finished as **runners-up.**

That same year, **2013,** she played for the **City West Falcons** in the

Liz played a big role in leading the Falcons to win the **2013 VNL Championship title,** and she was named the **Player of the Grand Final** for her **outstanding performance!**

Also in 2013, Liz captained the **Victorian Flames** in the

Her **leadership** and **skill** shone through, and under her captaincy **the Flames** came **third in the league!**

COMMENDABLE EFFORT!

And she was named **Flames MVP** for the season!

So many **ACHIEVEMENTS** in just one year!

VICTORIAN NETBALL LEAGUE

A **state-level competition** for teams from **Victoria**

Organised by **Netball Victoria**

Has **12** clubs

A feeder league for the **Victorian Suncorp Super Netball** teams **Melbourne Vixens** and **Collingwood Magpies**

VNL's most successful team, **City West Falcons,** have won **seven Championship titles** and **17 premierships** in total

AUSTRALIAN NETBALL CHAMPIONSHIPS

- Formerly the **Australian Netball League**
- Has **eight** clubs
- Organised by **Netball Australia**
- An **Australia-wide** competition
- Teams are considered the **reserve teams** of **Suncorp Super Netball teams** or the **representative teams** of **state netball leagues**

NETBALL AUSTRALIA'S HALL OF FAME LEGENDS

People in the **top tier** in the **Hall of Fame** have **LEGEND** status. This means they have **influenced the development of netball** at a national and international level. It's one of the **highest honours in Australian netball.**

LEGEND #1
Joyce Brown OAM
Captained Australia at the first World Netball Championships in 1963 and won a gold medal.

LEGEND #2
Margaret Pewtress OAM
Was a player, coach and selector, and a key administrator of the game.

LEGEND #3
Anne Sargeant OAM
One of the first inductees into the Australian Netball Hall of Fame.

LEGEND #4
Wilma Shakespear AM
Represented Australia at the 1963 World Netball Championships and won a gold medal.

LEGEND #5
Christine Burton OAM
A silver medallist at the
1967 and 1975 World
Championships.
LEGEND #6
Jill Mcintosh AM
Won the gold medal at the 1983
World Netball Championships and
helped the Australian team win four
gold medals as a coach.

CHAPTER FIVE

SHOOTING FOR THE STARS

Liz had her first introduction to **elite netball in 2014.**

She was invited to train with the **MELBOURNE VIXENS** during the preseason program as a **substitute,** but her big opportunity came when **midcourter Elissa Kent** had to take a break to have a baby.

‘I wasn’t thinking I would be a Vixen, I wasn’t thinking I would get any court time, I definitely didn’t think I would end up a **premiership player with the club!’**

LIZ WATSON

Liz joined the squad as a **permanent member** and wasted no time proving herself. She played a **key role** in the

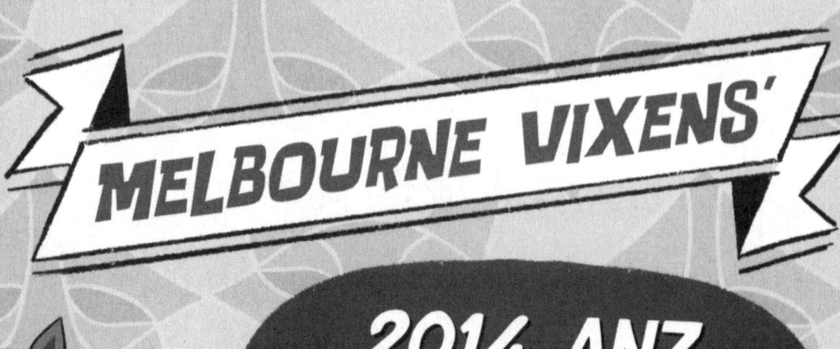

and earned the title of

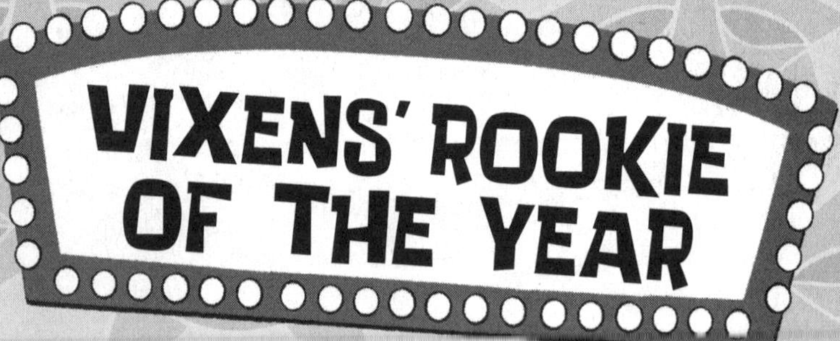

From that moment on, **Liz's career skyrocketed.** She became a **standout midcourter,** playing both **wing attack (WA)** and **centre (C).**
WA

LEGENDARY GAME

 WHO?

Melbourne Vixens v
Queensland Firebirds

 WHAT?

Final, 2014 ANZ Championship

 WHERE?

Hisense Arena, Melbourne

WHY WAS IT LEGENDARY?

The **Vixens were crowned Premiers of the ANZ Championship** for the **second time** in 2014. The Vixens led by just two goals at three-quarter time before going on to win 53–42!

'What I was **really proud of as captain** was seeing all of these young players just **own the moment** and **stand their own ground** out there on court.'

BIANCA CHATFIELD,
captain of the Melbourne Vixens 2008–2015

Did you know that on the same day that Liz was making her **surprise debut** for the **Melbourne Vixens,** her older brother **Matthew** was opening his **AFL season** with Carlton in Ballarat?

MELBOURNE VIXENS

The **Melbourne Vixens** is **Netball Victoria's** representative team competing in Australia's national netball competition, **Suncorp Super Netball.**

Year established: 2008

Home stadium: John Cain Arena

Official uniform colours: Jade, crimson and navy

ANC reserve team: Victorian Fury

Premierships: Suncorp Super Netball

Winners: 2020

Minor Premierships:
2017, 2020, 2022

ANZ Championship Winners:
2009, 2014

Runners Up: 2012

Minor Premierships:
2009, 2012, 2014

Prominent Members:
Liz Watson, Sharelle McMahon, Madison Browne, Bianca Chatfield, Kate Moloney, Geva Mentor, Catherine Cox

'This is definitely the **highest level** I've ever played at, and it's just so much more **intense** – the **pace** of the game and the **physicality** is just another **level up.**'
LIZ WATSON

CHAPTER SIX

WE ARE THE VIXENS

In 2017, the **ANZ CHAMPIONSHIP** became the

SUPER NETBALL LEAGUE

That same year, Liz was on the **Vixens team** that **won the first ever Suncorp Super Netball (SSN),** finishing as **minor premiers.**

Her efforts were recognised with the **SSN Young Star Award,** given to the best player under 23.

‘She’s never been a flashy player, but I love the fact that she’s come in, and she’s taken hold of the **opportunity** that she got. She **trains hard,** she contributes as much as she can to the team, she’s so **humble,** and **mature** far beyond her years. Just no fuss.’

BIANCA CHATFIELD,
captain of the Melbourne Vixens
2008–2015

Liz Ellis (AO) is one of **Australia's most successful netball players.** Her career highlights include captaining the Diamonds, three **World Championship** gold medals, two **Commonwealth Games** gold medals and four **national premierships.**

She is the **most capped** international player in Australia, having **played over 120 games for the Diamonds!**

THE LIZ ELLIS DIAMOND

is an award created in **2008** to **honour her achievements.**

This award is given to **Australia's top netball player.** It's the highest individual honour in Australian netball and recognises all the **hard work** and **dedication** that goes into **playing netball at the highest level.**

Liz Watson won this award in **2018** and **2022**! What a **LEGEND!**

By 2020, Liz had gone from **nervous debutant** to **superstar co-captain** of the Vixens! Alongside **midcourter Kate Moloney,** she led her team to another **premiership win,** this time in

SUNCORP SUPER NETBALL

'My Vixens journey so far has been **better than I could have ever imagined.** As a young girl playing netball you can only **dream** of one day being on the **biggest stage** playing the game that you love.'

LIZ WATSON

Unfortunately, in 2021, a **bone injury** in her foot forced her to miss the entire season. But like the **CHAMPION** she is, Liz worked hard to recover and made a **successful return** to the court in 2022.

By the time Liz left the **Melbourne Vixens,** she had played **134 games** for them over **ten seasons!**

AWARDS & HONOURS

NETBALL WORLD CUP

Winners: 2023

Runners Up: 2019

COMMONWEALTH GAMES

Winners: 2022

Runners Up: 2018

CONSTELLATION CUP

Winners: 2016, 2017, 2018, 2019, 2023

Runners Up: 2021, 2024

NETBALL QUAD SERIES

Winners: 2012, 2016, 2017, 2018 (x2), 2019, 2022, 2023, 2024

Runners Up: 2017

SUNCORP SUPER NETBALL

Winners: 2020

Minor Premierships: 2017, 2020

ANZ CHAMPIONSHIP

Winners: 2014

Minor Premierships: 2014

VICTORIAN NETBALL LEAGUE

Winners: 2013

AUSTRALIAN NATIONAL NETBALL CHAMPIONSHIPS

Winners: Under 19 (2012)

Runners Up: Under 21 (2013)

2013: Victorian Flames Most Valuable Player

2014: Vixens' Rookie of the Year

2015: Sport Australia Hall of Fame Scholarship & Mentoring Program Recipient

2017: Sharelle McMahon Medal

Rebel Rookie of the Year

Suncorp Super Netball Young Star Award

Suncorp Super Netball Team of the Year

2018: Sharelle McMahon Medal

Suncorp Super Netball Team of the Year

Liz Ellis Diamond

Australian International Player of the Year

2019: Suncorp Super Netball Team of the Year

2020: Suncorp Super Netball Team of the Year

2022: Liz Ellis Diamond

Suncorp Super Netball Team of the Year

Australian International Player of the Year

2023: VIS Award of Excellence

2024: Sunshine Coast Lightning Most Valuable Player

CHAPTER SEVEN

NETBALL KNOW-HOW

Netball is played by **two teams** of **seven players,** with each trying to keep or gain **possession** of the ball.

Each player wears a **bib** or **fabric patches** with their **position letters** on it.

Games are played on a **rectangular court** with **raised goal rings** at each end.

The aim of the game is to **score the most goals** in a game. Goals are scored by **shooting** the ball into the **correct net** at the end of the court.

Games run for **60 minutes** with **4 x 15-minute quarters** and a **break at half-time.**

The **umpire** does a **coin toss** to decide who starts with the ball.

Stay in the **designated areas** for your **position.**

Running with the ball is **not allowed,** but you can **pivot** on your landing foot or take **one additional step.**

Be at least **90cm away** from the player with the ball when **defending,** otherwise you get a **penalty.**

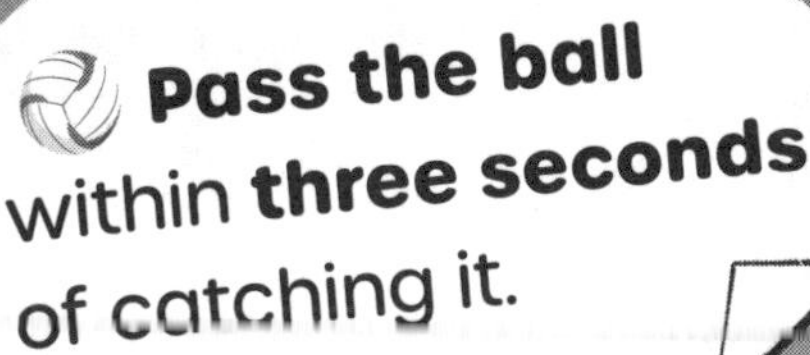

Pass the ball within **three seconds** of catching it.

Don't physically **contact** or **run into** other players, otherwise it's another **penalty.**

Only the **Goal Shooter** and **Goal Attack** can **score goals.**

Make sure someone in **each third** touches the ball.

NETBALL

WA

GS

GA

COURT

GD

C

GK

WD

There are **SEVEN playing positions** in a netball team.

GOAL SHOOTER (GS)
Scores goals and works in and around the circle with the GA. Must stay in the attacking third.

WING ATTACK (WA)
Sets up shooting opportunities for the GA and GS. Can go in the centre third and attacking third but not their goal circle.

CENTRE (C)
Takes the centre pass to start the game and links the defence and attack. Can go anywhere except the goal circles.

GOAL ATTACK (GA)

Works with the GS and scores goals. Allowed in the centre third and attacking third, including their goal circle.

WING DEFENCE (WD)

Makes interceptions and prevents the WA from feeding the ball into the circle. Allowed in the centre third and defensive third, excluding their goal circle.

GOAL DEFENCE (GD)

Tries to stop shooting opportunities and win the ball back. Allowed in the centre third and defensive third, including their goal circle.

GOAL KEEPER (GK)

Works with the GD to prevent the GA and GS from scoring goals. Only allowed in their defensive goal third and goal circle.

FAST FACTS

Netball was **adapted from basketball** in **1892** in the **United States** so female students could play something similar while wearing their **long skirts** and **full-sleeved shirts.**

Netball became a **'recognised' sport** of the **International Olympic Committee** in **1995,** but it hasn't yet been played at the **Summer Olympics.**

Netball was played at the **Commonwealth Games** for the first time in **1998** in **Kuala Lumpur. Australia** won the **Gold medal, New Zealand Silver** and **England** the **Bronze!**

Globally, over **20 million people** play netball in over **80 countries.** There are more than **70 national teams** across **five global regions.**

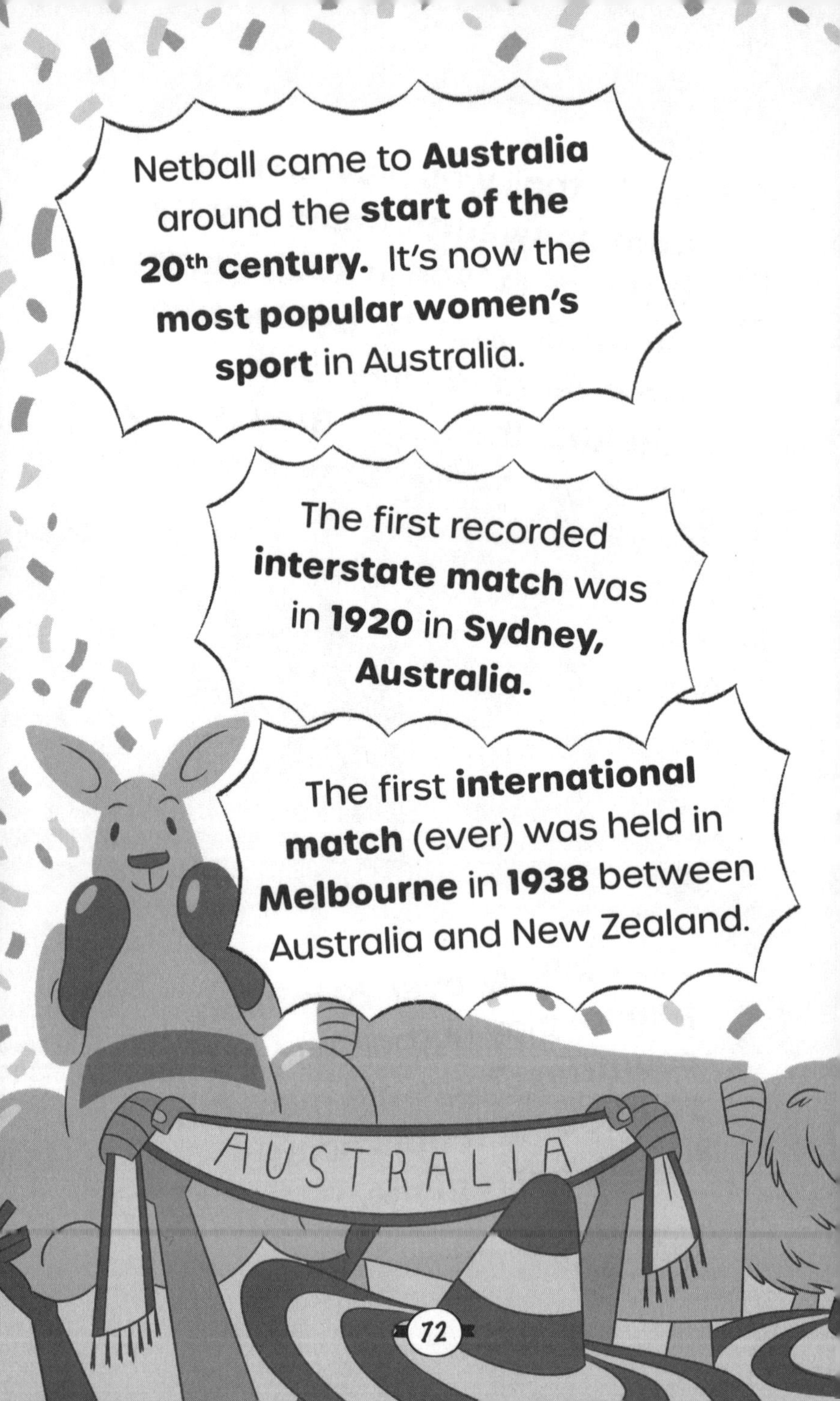
Netball came to Australia around the start of the 20th century. It's now the most popular women's sport in Australia.
The first recorded interstate match was in 1920 in Sydney, Australia.
The first international match (ever) was held in Melbourne in 1938 between Australia and New Zealand.
AUSTRALIA

AUSTRALIA WON!

Australia won the **inaugural Netball World Cup in 1963,** and since then has won the **most titles.**

GO AUSSIE

DID YOU KNOW...?

In **1931,** the **All-Australian Women's Basketball Association** said players had to be **silent** during the game because it wasn't **'lady-like'** to **call for the ball** or **shout encouragement** to teammates.

Can you imagine playing a game of netball in silence? Luckily, that rule didn't last long!

CHAPTER EIGHT

DIAMONDS ARE FOREVER

Liz's **rise was extremely quick** since her Vixens debut in 2014. After just **seven senior games** with the Victorian team, she was **selected for the Australian national squad** that same year.

'I still **can't believe I'm in the Diamonds squad.** I don't even know how to explain it; it's just **one of those moments that I'll never forget.**'

LIZ WATSON

However, she had to **wait until 2016** for her **first appearance** on the court when she **came off the bench at three quarter time** against Liverpool in England.

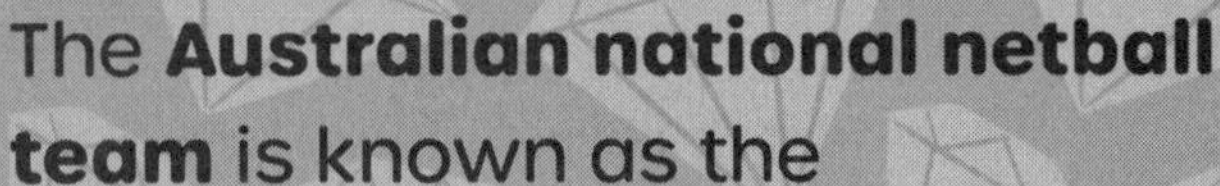

The **Australian national netball team** is known as the

AUSTRALIAN DIAMONDS

Even though the team has been around since **the 1930s,** the nickname was only officially adopted in **2008.**

Did you know that the Australian women's **basketball team** nickname is **also** a **gemstone?** They're known as the **OPALS!**

DIAMONDS FACTS

The Diamonds represent Australia in **international netball tournaments** such as:

- **the Constellation Cup**
- **the Netball World Cup**
- **the Netball Quad Series**
- **the Commonwealth Games**
- **the Fast 5 Netball World Series**
- **the World Games**

CONSTELLATION CUP

The **Constellation Cup** is an **international netball competition** between **Australia** and **New Zealand.** Every year, the two teams play a series of **test matches** across both countries.

The tournament is named after the **Southern Cross constellation** which is on the **flags** of both **Australia** and **New Zealand.**

The **trophy** is made from **sterling silver** and is encrusted with **101 diamonds,** so it shines bright just like the stars!

First season: 2010
Australia's titles: 11
New Zealand's titles: 3

LEGENDARY GAME

WHO?

Diamonds v Silver Ferns

WHAT?

Fourth Test, 2016 Constellation Cup

WHERE?

Stadium Southland, Invercargill, New Zealand

WHY WAS IT LEGENDARY?

Having won **two of the previous three tests,** the **Diamonds** started strong, but the **Silver Ferns** fought back to trail by two goals with one minute on the clock. The Diamonds scored **two late goals in the last 30 seconds to win 49–45!**

SILVER FERNS

'The **defensive pressure** the **Silver Ferns** put on tonight was **pretty phenomenal.** They were having a fly at the ball, confusing space, and **they were doing a great job.**'

CLARE MCMENIMAN,
captain of the Diamonds 2016

LEGENDARY GAME

WHO?

Diamonds v Silver Ferns

WHAT?

Fourth Test, 2023
Constellation Cup

WHERE?

Spark Arena, Auckland,
New Zealand

WHY WAS IT LEGENDARY?

Australia won the first two tests and were ready to **dominate.** However, New Zealand won the third and fourth tests! It was going to be a **draw,** but the **Diamonds** had a **better aggregate score** (the sum of the two matches they won) and were **declared the winners. Phew!**

'It was one of the **best experiences** I've had, especially the Constellation Cup. We were up against New Zealand, so I guess **number one and two in the world.**'

LIZ WATSON

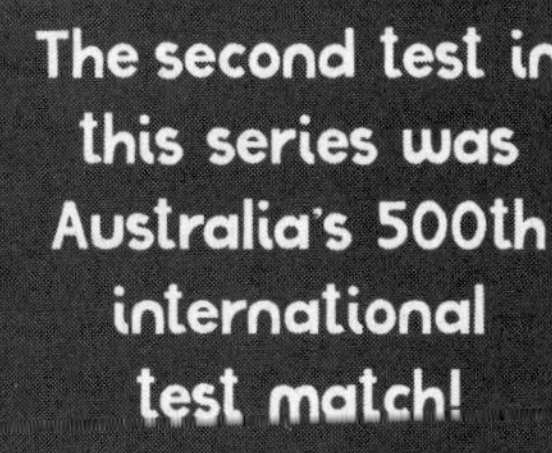

NETBALL QUAD SERIES

The **Netball Quad Series** is an annual international netball competition between **Australia, New Zealand, England** and **South Africa.**

First season: 2012
Australia's titles: 9
New Zealand wins: 2

The **first ever tournament** was played in **2012** across Australia and New Zealand.

AUSTRALIA WON!

LEGENDARY GAME

WHO?

Diamonds v Silver Ferns

WHAT?

Round 3, 2018
Netball Quad Series

WHERE?

Ellis Park Arena, Johannesburg, South Africa

WHY WAS IT LEGENDARY?

The Diamonds were **ruthless** from the start and pulled off a **67–48 victory** – the biggest win over the Silver Ferns since 2012 (at the time). **Australia won the series,** and on top of that, Liz was named **Most Valuable Player** of the match!

'They should be **extraordinarily pleased** with themselves, they **represented** our country and netball in Australia with discretion.'

LISA ALEXANDER,
coach of the Diamonds
2011–2020

NETBALL'S GREATEST RIVALS

The **Australian Diamonds** and the **New Zealand Silver Ferns** have a **long-standing rivalry** that first started in **1938,** when they played each other in the **world's first international match.**

Since then, the two teams like to battle over the **no.1** and **no.2** spots in the rankings. Right now, **Australia is in the lead!**

CURRENT WORLD RANKINGS

1	Australia
2	New Zealand
3	Jamaica
4	England
5	South Africa
6	Uganda
7	Malawi
8	Tonga
9	Wales
10	Scotland

Legendary Snack

Liz's go-to pre-match snack is **banana, peanut butter and honey on toast.** Some of her other **favourite recipes** include...

Apple doughnuts

Choc, date and coconut balls

Apricot, nut and seed slice

Rainbow porridge

CHAPTER NINE

GOING FOR GOLD

CAPTAIN'S CALL

Liz stayed on **top of her game** each season. Everyone thought she was **one of the best WAs** in the game, so it was no surprise when Liz was named the **25th national captain** of the **Diamonds** in **2021.**

'Liz's **passion** and **drive** for **success** is evident and she has a fantastic ability to stay calm whilst continuing to **empower players** around her.'

STACEY MARINKOVICH,
head coach of the Diamonds

'I am very **humbled** and **proud** to be acknowledged by my teammates. **I love this sport, I love this team and I love this country.** To be given the **honour** as captain of the Australian Diamonds is something I will forever be grateful for.'

LIZ WATSON

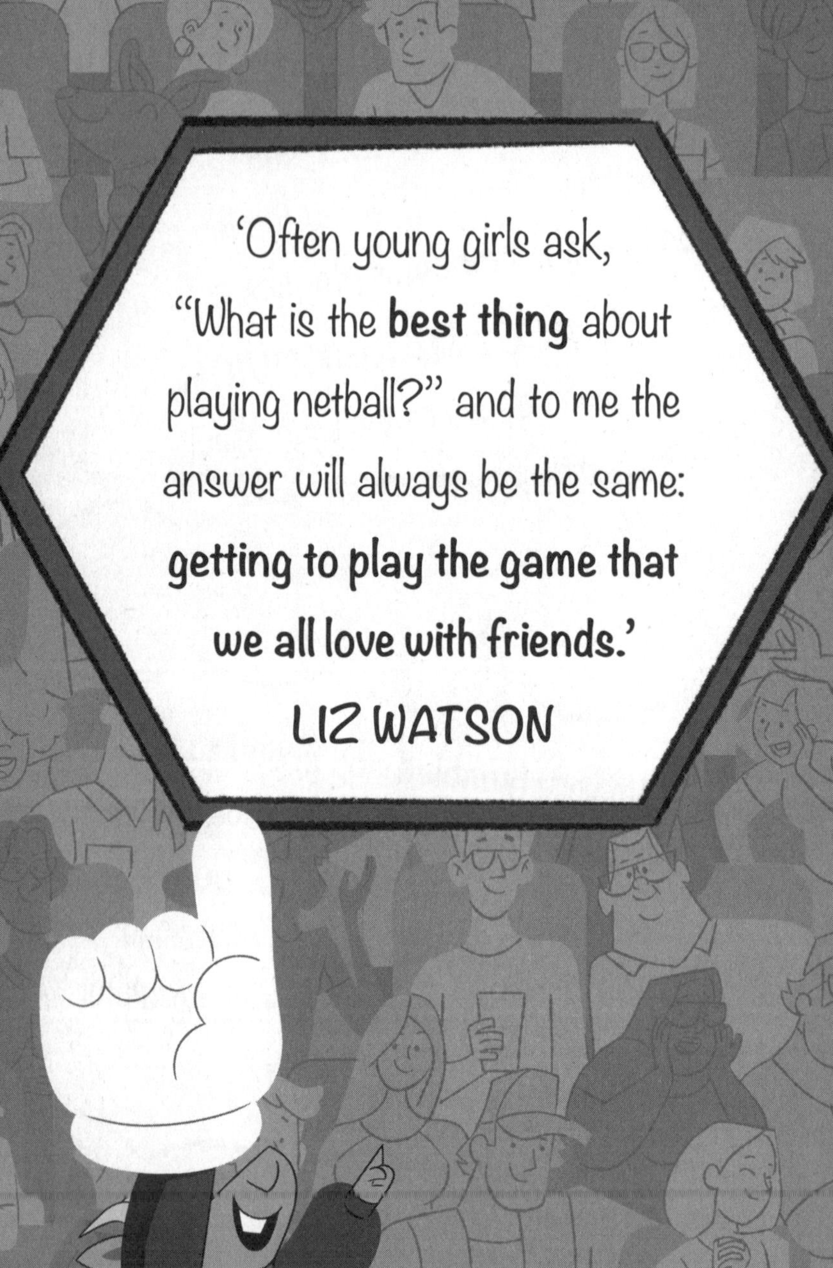

‘Often young girls ask, “What is the **best thing** about playing netball?” and to me the answer will always be the same: **getting to play the game that we all love with friends.**’

LIZ WATSON

Liz has become **very close friends** with many of her **teammates** over the years, such as...

The Commonwealth Games is one of netball's **biggest tournaments!**

Ever since playing each other in the first **demonstration match in 1990, Australia** and **New Zealand** have been the top teams to beat.

In fact, Australia won **gold** in **1998, 2002, 2014** and **2022,** and have the **most titles** out of all the teams that compete.

LEGENDARY GAME

WHO?

Diamonds v Jamaica

WHAT?

Gold medal match, 2022 Commonwealth Games

WHERE?

National Exhibition Centre, Birmingham, England

WHY WAS IT LEGENDARY?

It was a **nail-biting match,** but the Diamonds celebrated a **55–51 victory** over **Jamaica.** This was Liz's **second time** playing at the Commonwealth Games, the Diamonds' first major tournament victory in **seven years** AND Australia's **1000th Commonwealth Games gold medal! WOW!**

'She's [Liz] probably won **every single individual award** that you can imagine except for a gold medal at a major tournament, so if they could win it that would be the **cherry on top of her career so far.'**

MANUELA WATSON

THE NETBALL WORLD CUP

The **Netball World Cup** is the **biggest tournament** in netball! Every **four years,** the best teams from around the world compete to be **crowned champions.**

The Diamonds have battled fierce rivals like **New Zealand** and **England** in many exciting finals, but they are the **most successful team ever, winning 12 World Cups!**

England, Australia, Jamaica, New Zealand, Trinidad & Tobago, Singapore, Scotland, South Africa

And Australia
again in 2027!

LEGENDARY GAME

WHO?

Diamonds v England

WHAT?

Gold Medal match, 2023
Netball World Cup

WHERE?

Cape Town International
Convention Centre, South Africa

WHY WAS IT LEGENDARY?

The Diamonds reclaimed the **World Cup** and proved they are the **world's best netball team** with a **61-45 win over England.** This win meant that **Australia** held **every major title** in world netball that season!

'This group was just so focused, so determined – every single one of us. I just knew there was **no stopping us.** We had the same feeling last year at Comm Games. I was like, **we're winning today.'**
LIZ WATSON

BALL BASICS

There are **two main sizes** of netballs available:

SIZE FOUR NETBALLS

- For players under ten
- Are a smaller size

SIZE FIVE NETBALLS

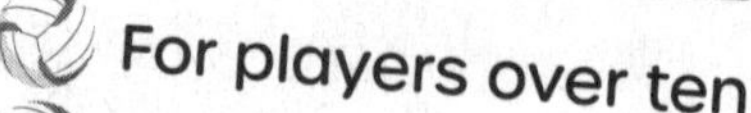

- For players over ten
- Are a full size
- Should be between 680 and 710 mm in circumference
- Should weigh between 400 and 450 grams

DID YOU KNOW
the first netballs were **brown** and made from **leather?**

CHAPTER TEN

THE ROAD AHEAD

Liz still has a **lot of playing** to do!

After the 2023 season, **Liz left the Melbourne Vixens** and signed a **three-year deal** with the

She debuted for her new club in the 2024 season in the **WA position.**

'She brings a level of **competitiveness** but also a **calmness** [to our training environment], which is reflected in the way she has led on and off the court.'

BELINDA REYNOLDS,
head coach of Sunshine Coast Lightning

She remains **captain of the Diamonds** heading into the 2025 season and is no doubt preparing her team to win at the **Netball World Cup in 2027.** The tournament will be played in **Sydney, Australia!**

Things Liz

- Reading
- Baking

- The colour purple
- The thumbs-up emoji

Watson loves

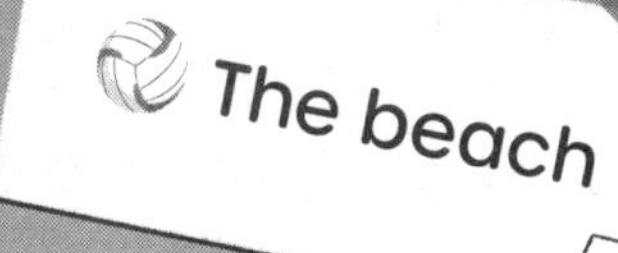

Being active

Liz **loves to train** and **play netball,** but she does her best to find time to do **things outside of netball** throughout the season, such as...

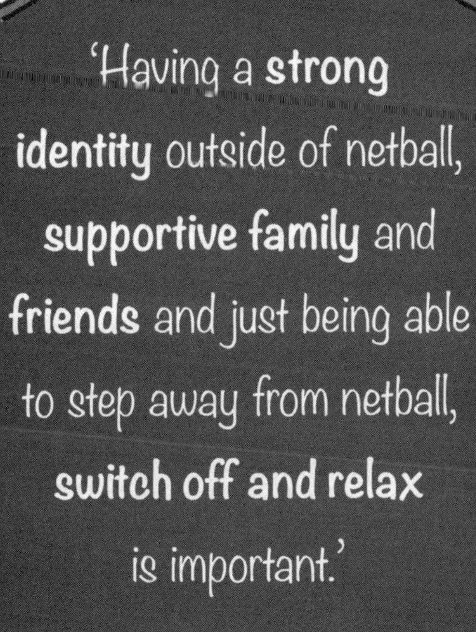
'Having a **strong identity** outside of netball, **supportive family** and **friends** and just being able to step away from netball, **switch off and relax** is important.'
LIZ WATSON

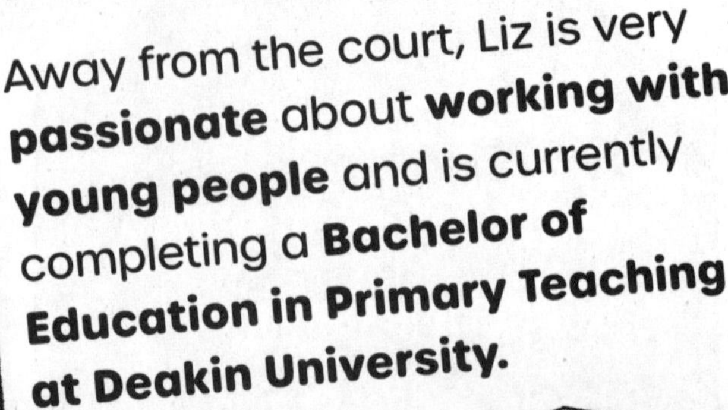

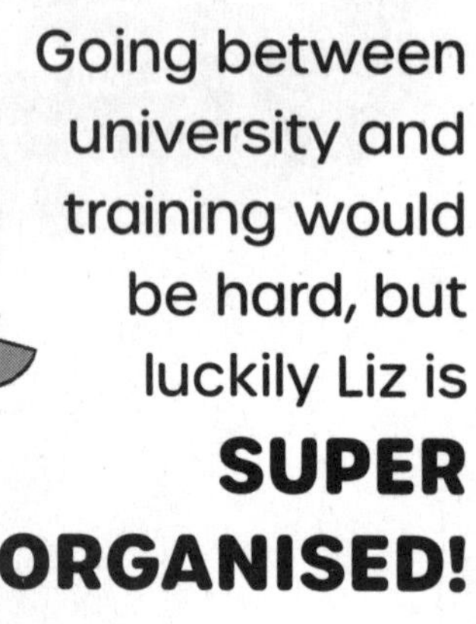

Going between university and training would be hard, but luckily Liz is **SUPER ORGANISED!**

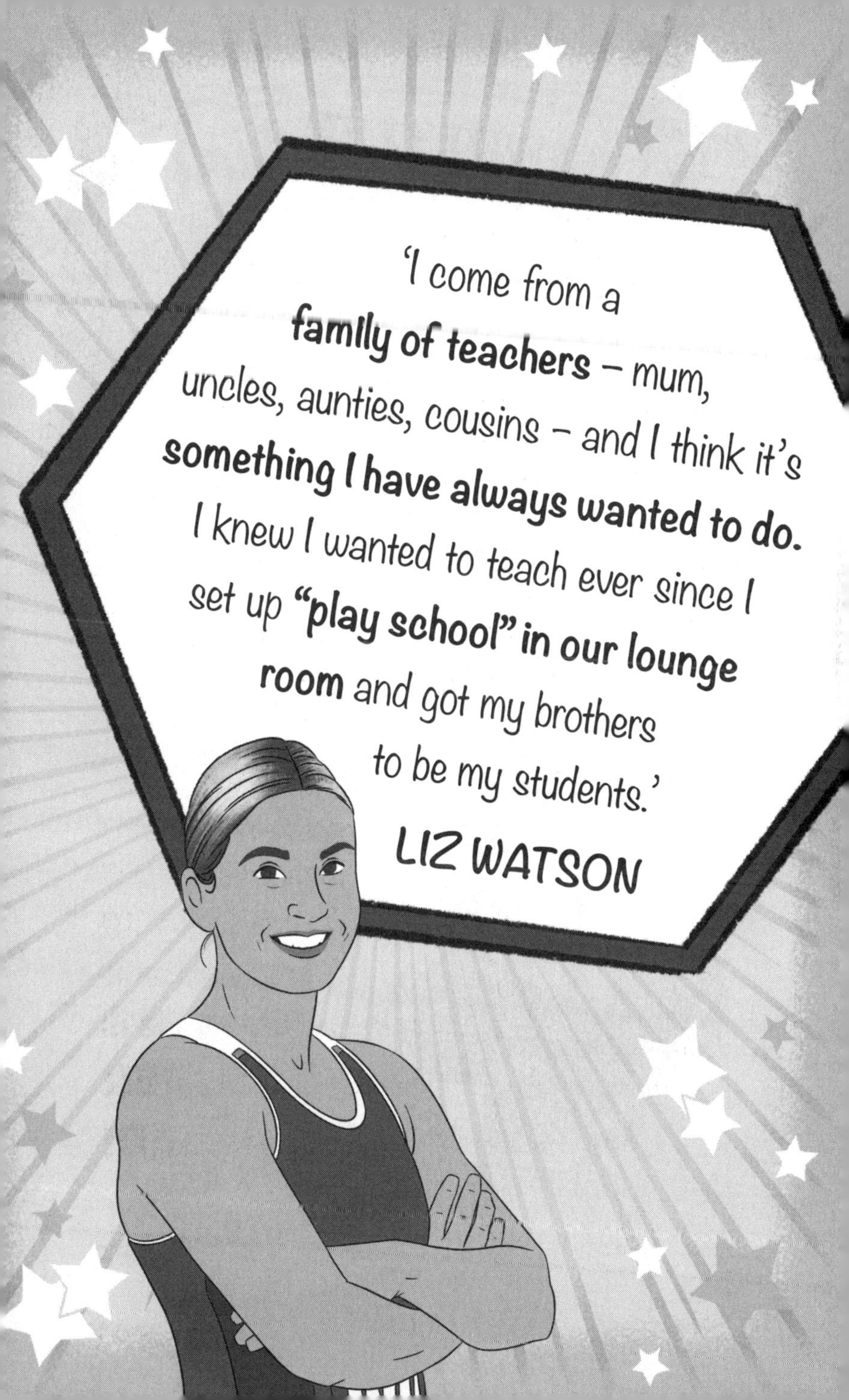
'I come from a **family of teachers** – mum, uncles, aunties, cousins – and I think it's **something I have always wanted to do.** I knew I wanted to teach ever since I set up **"play school" in our lounge room** and got my brothers to be my students.'
LIZ WATSON

THE LEGENDARY LIZ WATSON
2 GOLD MEDALS
33
2 SILVER MEDALS
106 SSN APPEARANCES

91 TEST CAPS

5 SELECTIONS FOR SSN TEAM OF THE YEAR

134 MELBOURNE VIXENS APPEARANCES

No doubt about it, **Liz Watson** is a true

SPORTING LEGEND!

1. In what Australian city was Liz born?
2. Which two positions does Liz play?
3. How far away from a player do you need to be when defending?
4. Name three sports (aside from netball) Liz played when she was a child?

5. In what year did Liz debut for the Melbourne Vixens?

6. The Melbourne Vixens won the ANZ Championship In 2014. What was the score?

7. How long is a netball game?

8. Which country has won the most Netball World Cups?

9. Which two positions can shoot goals?

10. What is the Australian national netball team called?

ANSWERS:
1. Carlton, Victoria **2.** Centre and Wing Attack **3.** At least 90 cm **4.** Footy, swimming, basketball, tennis or athletics **5.** 2014 **6.** 53-42 **7.** 60 minutes **8.** Australia **9.** Goal Shooter and Goal Attack **10.** Australian Diamonds

Held ball: When you have possession of the ball for more than three seconds without passing it.

Contact: Any action that results in players touching or bumping into each other. It can be accidental or deliberate.

Bounce pass: When you bounce the ball to your teammate. It's commonly used in the goal circle to get around tall defenders.

Pivot: When you plant one foot on the ground and move the other foot around the body in a circular motion.

Here if you need: A common phrase that tells your teammate that you're in position to support if they need to pass the ball.

Netball Ready Position (NRP): Describes the best way to position your body to be ready for action on court: on the balls of your feet, knees bent and eyes facing forward.

Feeding: When you pass the ball into the goal circle from outside the ring.

Intercept: When you regain possession of the ball during a pass by the opposition. You need speed and a good defensive awareness to pull this off!

Offside: When a player goes into an area they are not allowed in.

Airborne throw: When you catch and release the ball before your feet return to the court.

Feint pass: When you aim a ball pass in one direction and then release it into a completely different area.

Pickup: When a player gains possession of a loose ball on the ground. This usually happens after a bad pass, deflection or bad catch.

More FACTS, more STATS, more LEGENDS!

legendsofsportbooks.com.au